THE INTERVIEWER –
LUCINDA SALLIS

Lucinda Sallis used to work in public relations until 2003 when she went to Afghanistan with an aid organisation to work as a Finance Officer. She joined Medecins Sans Frontieres in the spring of 2004 and was based for nearly a year in the Nuba Mountains, Sudan working as a logistician/administrator. Lucinda worked side by side with Carbino. She is now with MSF in Indonesia.

Medecins Sans Frontieres (MSF) is an international humanitarian aid organisation that provides emergency medical assistance to populations in danger in more than 80 countries. MSF works in rehabilitation of hospitals and dispensaries, vaccination programmes and water and sanitation projects. MSF also works in remote health care centres, slum areas and provides training of local personnel. All this is done with the objective of rebuilding health structures to acceptable levels.

THE INTERVIEW PROCESS

The interview was conducted by Lucinda Sallis, the MSF log-administrator in Nuba. Lucinda had lived and worked with Carbino for nearly a year during which time they became very close. They managed to book a few hours off work one afternoon (not so easy here where people work seven-day weeks and Carbino is frequently away on outreach) to sit in the shade and for Carbino to tell his story. At first Carbino found it difficult. People are not used to talking in detail about their suffering in this part of the world and he was generally very dismissive of what he went through. But Lucinda knew him well and managed to coax the details out of him.

CO ... KT-176-774

Carbino with Lucinda (far left) and Rivkah an MSF outreach nurse.

Introduction

Around the world today 17 million people are living far from the place where they would choose to be. Many have been driven from their homes by natural disasters or by the need to find food during times of famine. Others have been forced from their communities or countries by persecution or government oppression. Millions have fled their homes or countries to escape wars that endanger, or threaten to endanger, their lives.

WHAT IS A REFUGEE?

When ordinary people leave their homes under these circumstances they become refugees. Some seek safety over the border in a neighbouring country. Others move from one part of their country to another and are described as internally-displaced persons (IDPs). In this book, the word refugee describes both people seeking safety in another country and internally-displaced people.

THE HAZARDS OF WAR

During times of war, innocent civilians are often caught up in the fighting. They may be killed or injured, and their homes and livelihoods may be destroyed. In many recent wars, an official, uniformed government army fights rebel forces. In these cases it may be hard for government forces to tell rebel soldiers apart from civilians, leading to civilian casualties and deaths. Sometimes, the people may support the rebels by providing food, shelter and information. If so, the government forces may try to stop this support by attacking ordinary people.

SEEKING SAFETY

It is not an easy decision to leave your home, your livelihood and perhaps some of your family. People will often stay put, take shelter and hope

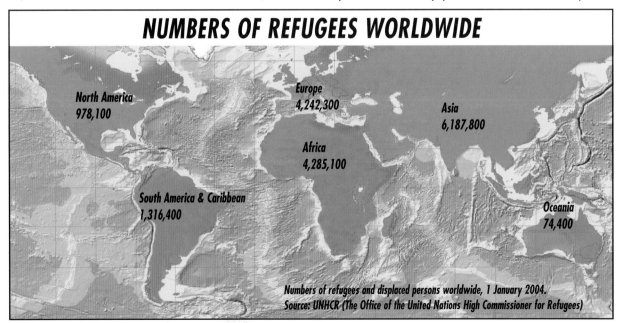

NUMBERS OF REFUGEES WORLDWIDE

North America
978,100

Europe
4,242,300

Asia
6,187,800

Africa
4,285,100

South America & Caribbean
1,316,400

Oceania
74,400

Numbers of refugees and displaced persons worldwide, 1 January 2004.
Source: UNHCR (The Office of the United Nations High Commissioner for Refugees)

real-life stories

REFUGEE CAMP

Carbino's Story

by David Dalton

Produced in association with

Médecins sans Frontières (MSF)

WE WOULD LIKE TO THANK THE FOLLOWING FOR THEIR HELP IN THE PRODUCTION OF THIS BOOK:

Petrana Ford and Lucinda Sallis from Medecins Sans Frontieres

*Clare Graham and Ahmed Momoh of UNHCR, the Office of the United Nations
High Commissioner for Refugees,
Jean Coppendale and Indexing Specialists (UK) Ltd;*

and our special thanks to

Carbino

without whom this book would not have been possible.

9 September, 2004: Sudanese refugees flee from the Darfur region of Sudan into neighbouring Chad, to escape the fighting between rebels and government forces.

that the fighting passes. However, sooner or later, they realise that they can only find safety by leaving the area of fighting. People take what they think they will need, and what they can carry. They walk away from their homes, their fields and perhaps the unburied bodies of their loved ones, not knowing when they will be able to return.

Some refugees may find safety, especially if they cross a border into a neighbouring country. The government of the neighbouring country may set up a refugee camp and protect the people in the camp. But if the refugees are internally displaced, they may not be safe for long. Fighting may break out in their new location or they may be targeted by one of the armies involved in the war.

TIMELINE OF WAR IN SUDAN

1956: Sudan becomes independent. Civil war begins in the south led by the Anya Nya movement.

1972: Under the Addis Ababa peace agreement between the Anya Nya and the Sudanese government, the south becomes a self-governing region.

1978: Oil is discovered in Bentiu, southern Sudan.

1983: The president of Sudan, President Numayri, declares the introduction of Sharia law (Islamic law). Civil war breaks out again in the south involving government forces and the Sudan People's Liberation Army (SPLA), led by John Garang.

1985: President Numayri is deposed and Sharia law is abolished when a new regime takes over the government.

1991: A revolution in Sudan's neighbour Ethiopia brings down the ruling regime, which supported the SPLA. Sudanese refugees are forced to return to Sudan. Sharia law re-introduced, but not applied to all southern states. After 1991, conflict also breaks out between different factions of the southern forces.

1999: Sudan begins to export oil.

JUNE 2001: Failure of Nairobi peace talks between the president of Sudan President Umar al-Bashir (who took power in 1989) and rebel leader John Garang.

The timeline continues on page 7.

Sudan is the biggest country in Africa, with an area of 2.5 million sq km – more than ten times the size of the UK. The country is divided into 26 states. (Inset map of Africa with Sudan highlighted).

SUDAN – A COUNTRY AT WAR

Over the past 50 years, Sudan, in Africa, has been torn apart by civil war. Years of conflict between the Sudanese government and rebel groups has created one of the world's worst humanitarian and refugee crises.

SUDAN – A BRIEF HISTORY

Sudan gained its present borders as a British colony at the end of the 19th century. As was the case with many countries in Africa, the borders established by European colonists brought together people who had little in common. In the north of Sudan, the people are Muslims, many of them Arabic-speaking and ethnically Arab. In the south, the people are Black, Christian or Animist, and speak a variety of languages.

INDEPENDENCE

In 1956, Sudan became independent. The new government was based in the capital city of Khartoum and was dominated by people from the north of the country, who encouraged economic development in the north, along the irrigated valley of the River Nile.

Following independence, the people of the south wanted autonomy – to be able to run their own region themselves. They also wanted to have their share of economic development and to be able to use their own languages in their schools, courts and government. In 1956, the south rebelled against the government in Khartoum.

THE FIRST CIVIL WAR

The first Sudanese civil war, between the southern Anya Nya movement and the government in the north lasted 17 years. In 1972, under the Addis Ababa peace agreement, the people of the south were given more power over their own affairs.

SUDAN – FACTS

- *Population (July 2004 estimate): 39,148,162*
- *Ethnic groups: Arabs 60%, Dinka 12%, Beja 7%, others 21%*
- *Languages: Arabic 60%, 115 languages are spoken in the south*
- *Religions: Islam 70%, Animist 26%, Christianity 4%*
- *Average life expectancy male: 57 years*
- *Average life expectancy female: 59 years*
- *Number of doctors per 100,000 people: 16*
- *Capital city: Khartoum*
- *Currency: 1dinar = 10 Sudanese pounds*

Fighters of the Sudan People's Liberation Army (SPLA), some of them new recruits, train at a base in Sudan's Nuba Mountains region.

THE SECOND CIVIL WAR

For 11 years there was peace in Sudan, but many tensions still existed between the people of the south and the government in Khartoum. In 1983, when the government imposed Sharia law (Islamic law) throughout Sudan, including in the predominantly Christian south, civil war broke out again. This time the Sudan People's Liberation Army (SPLA), led by John Garang, fought against the government.

This new civil war soon settled into a deadlock, which neither side could win – government forces could hold the towns, but they could not control the countryside.

Over the next 21 years, up to 2 million people would die (including both soldiers and civilians) and over 7 million people would be internally displaced or become refugees in neighbouring countries. Today, hundreds of thousands of Sudanese people are still living in refugee camps waiting to go home.

TIMELINE OF WAR IN SUDAN

JANUARY 2002: The government and SPLA sign a landmark, six-month renewable ceasefire agreement for the central Nuba Mountains – a key rebel stronghold.

20/7/02: Government and SPLA sign Machakos Protocol on ending the 19-year civil war. The Sudanese government accepts the right of the south to seek self-determination after a six-year interim period.

27/7/02: Through the mediation of Ugandan President Yoweri Museveni, President al-Bashir and SPLA leader John Garang meet face-to-face for the first time.

OCTOBER 2002: The government and SPLA agree to a ceasefire for the duration of negotiations. Despite this, hostilities continue.

NOVEMBER 2002: Negotiations stall over allocation of civil service and government jobs, but both sides agree to observe ceasefire.

MAY 2004: The Sudanese government and SPLA make power-sharing agreements as part of a peace deal to end the civil war. The deal follows earlier breakthroughs on the division of oil and non-oil wealth.

JANUARY 2005: The Sudanese government and SPLA sign a peace deal to end the civil war. The agreement includes a permanent ceasefire and agreements on wealth and power sharing.

CHAPTER ONE: Meet Carbino

During the civil war in Sudan, 2 million children became refugees. Many fled the fighting with their families, but others, orphaned or separated from their parents, were forced to survive alone – Carbino was one of those children. For 14 years, he battled hunger, loss and terrible danger. This is Carbino's story of war in Sudan.

CARBINO SAYS ...

"My name is Carbino and I am 27 years old. I was born on 18 July, 1977. I was born in Panaru in Western Upper Nile in south Sudan. I am Dinka.

I'm not sure how to describe myself, you know. I get more of my description from other people living around me. They call me Lim Lim, which is very sweet, so I sound sweet to everybody around me. I really like to be a good friend to people, and I have an attitude of feeling sympathy for everybody, so I always sympathise with people.

I speak a few languages. One of the languages that I speak best is Dinka, which is my mother-tongue. I also speak English and Arabic, and I speak Swahili and Nuer, as well.

I like to entertain myself always. One of my favourite ways to entertain myself is by dancing if there is any music around, and also by telling stories or listening to stories told by people around me. Also, I like swimming, and I am a footballer, as well. I like kicking! I like African music – original music from Congo.

Carbino in January 2005 in the Nuba Mountains region of Sudan.

My favourite music is reggae funk from Bob Marley, I like those songs very much. One of my favourite books is Long Walk to Freedom *written by a famous man in Africa, Nelson Mandela.*

I feel really very proud to be asked to be in this book because it keeps history going. If my life story is recorded and written down, it might keep people reading it. Even my children in the future might read it, and I think it will keep my name existing in the time coming."

Refugee Nuba families shelter from the hot sun in the Nuba Mountains region of Sudan.

SUDAN – THE ENVIRONMENT

Sudan is a vast plain broken up by several mountain ranges. There are desert regions in the north and west, and areas of swamp and rainforest in the south. The River Nile flows northwards through Sudan, from its sources in Ethiopia and Uganda, to Egypt and the Mediterranean Sea. The climate in Sudan is hot all the year round, with one rainy season between May and September, when much of the land floods. But rainfall in Sudan is unreliable and droughts happen frequently.

THE PEOPLE OF SUDAN

There are over 300 different tribes in Sudan. The Dinka are the largest ethnic group in southern Sudan. About 2 million people speak the Dinka language. Many of the people of northern Sudan are nomadic livestock farmers, while further south, where there is more rainfall, the people are settled farmers. Many Sudanese men leave their families behind in their villages and travel to the cities or around the country to find farm or labouring work.

"I grew up in my village. My father was a farmer, he kept animals on his farm. I have two brothers – we are all boys in our family. Moses, he is 22 years old and James is 16 years. I used to take very good care of them, especially when my mum was not in the house, when she was working on the farm. My jobs were to look after small animals, the goats and calves, and sometimes I went for water. That was my daily work. My father had quite a lot of animals in our compound, maybe 87 or 89 calves, plus goats and sheep.

To describe our old house…there was a compound with some trees around it and our garden where we grew vegetables, like pumpkins and tomatoes, and sorghum (a type of grain) and corn. The compound was around three big tukuls. One for my mum, one for goods and the other one for my father. I normally slept with my father in his tukul. Inside the tukul we slept on mats and there was a place for a fire, for heating when it was cold. My uncles from our clan lived near us, so our house was not an isolated home. We were surrounded by relatives.

Our main food was made from sorghum plus milk, vegetables and sometimes meat. We normally had enough food. The cooking was my mum's job. We also gathered fruit, wild fruit, in the bush,

Carbino sits beside a tukul in the Nuba Mountains village where he now lives. Tukuls are huts made from locally available materials, such as thatch (dried grass), mud or stone.

In villages like the one where Carbino grew up, water is collected from hand-dug wells. In the dry season, when water supplies dry up, people may have to walk further afield to a water point.

because our village was surrounded by bush. Twice a week I visited one of the open-air markets within the village. No shops, just people selling things in an open air place. We had no running water and I never saw a TV in those days. No TV or radio, there was nothing. We did not have any kind of transport either – people used their legs, their strength to do things.

The village was surrounded by thorn bushes which the people depended on for construction and firewood. In the rainy season my village looked very nice because most of the people grew crops and created beauty on their pieces of ground.

The village was maybe 6,000 to 7,000 people. The whole village was Dinka."

DINKA FARMERS

The Dinka, and other tribes in southern Sudan, grow crops and raise herds of animals, especially cattle. They switch between crop-growing and cattle-grazing areas with the different seasons.

• Cattle are very important to Dinka people. They provide milk and meat, and their dried dung is used as a fuel for burning. In good years, the herds build up to provide a reserve for when drought occurs and crops fail. Then the people can sell cattle to buy grain, and survive the drought.

• During the dry season, the young men take the cattle to camps by the rivers, where the animals can find grazing and water to drink. Old and infirm people, and mothers with young children, stay in permanent villages surrounded by fields of a grain called sorghum.

• When the wet season comes round again, the grazing land by the rivers is flooded and everyone gathers in the villages on higher ground.

A young Dinka boy milks one of his family's cows.

11

"In the centre of the village we had a big playground where boys and girls came for recreations, like dancing and entertainment. Especially in the evening hours.

We played different kinds of games – one of the games was the crocodile game. This game is normally played in the rainy season when there is a lot of water. Young girls and boys go to a river and one boy or girl chooses to be a crocodile, and the rest of the people run away from him or her. If she or he manages to catch one of you, you are then on their side and you are also a crocodile. So we would chase each other the whole day until everybody involved was a crocodile. We played this in the river and that's where I learned to swim.

The biggest adventure I remember from when I was a child in my village was when we (Carbino and his friends) went to the bush and we found an antelope which was speared by somebody and it was half dead. It was a lucky day for us to get that, and we shared the meat together. I remember, two days after that came the time that we had to leave the land (the area where Carbino had grown up) to go to a different place. So my good adventure marked the end of my time in my home area.

The good thing about my community was that it was a community that loved to be together and share ideas together – always reaching to achieve a common goal, and maintaining our culture. I liked the way people respected each other, especially between the young children and the adults. Everybody knew his or her position. The way my community ruled itself was something very interesting. People ruled themselves, solving their own problems, and we created peace within the community.

Carbino remembers his village as full of animals – cows, donkeys and goats everywhere!

The bad thing about my community was that people didn't think much about different cultures. For instance, I lived in a village where there was no school, people neglected that. I didn't go to school. Maybe they could have gone from illiteracy to being people who are educated, but they never thought about that. It is harmful now to the younger generation who are in the region, because if the community could have thought to do something, to educate their children, maybe in this world there could be a bit of development, but it never happened.

No-one came from outside to our village. The first time I saw white people was early in 1982. They were explorers, I think. They came to look for oil in the area. To me it was very strange because I never saw a white person before. All the children in the village, plus me, were really scared to see such a people."

EDUCATION IN SUDAN

Only about one in three children go to school in Sudan. Of the 1.6 million children aged between 5 and 14 years in southern Sudan, only 18 per cent are in school. Education in Sudan is hampered by the country's poverty, and has suffered because of the wars. Schools have been destroyed; people have been forced away from their homes to refugee camps where there are no schools; and the government spends very little on education. In 1990, the government spent 0.9 per cent of the country's wealth on education, but 3.6 per cent on the war. As a result of years of neglect, many adults cannot read or write. The adult literacy rate is about 36 per cent in the north, and less than 15 per cent in the south. Throughout the country, many more boys than girls go to school.

FROM BOYS TO MEN

Dinka boys become young men in a ceremony that often includes cutting ritual scars into their foreheads. After this, the boys become the warriors who care for the cattle in the dry-season cattle camp. Young men often have favourite oxen; they make up songs about them and attach tassels to their horns or train their horns into special shapes. The young men must also defend the cattle from predators, and against raids by other tribes.

A young Dinka tribesman with ritual scars on his forehead. He wears an ivory earring and painted bead necklaces.

"There are a few things I can say about my Dinka culture. One of the biggest things Dinka have is what they call an initiation, a marking of childhood to adulthood. They start when you are 15 years old by putting a mark on your forehead. If they do this to you, it shows that you are mature and you can defend your community, and you can take care of your wife when you are married.

One of the special occasions I can remember from when I was young was an initiation time. People slaughtered a lot goats and cows to celebrate. They danced and people did wrestling and stick fighting for fun.

There was no church or temple in my village, but there was a place where people practised their traditions, like sacrificing to their gods. In our belief, people sacrifice twice a year to their gods, to keep their children healthy and to provide them with enough food and things like that.

Dinka beliefs are a little bit strange because people worship and believe in gods, like snakes. Certain communities have a strong belief in a certain snake, like the cobra, and when you visit their house, maybe you can find the cobra laying around with people. The people adore the snakes and they worship them. They say the snakes are

Wrestling is a traditional pastime in Dinka culture. Wrestlers compete to entertain spectators, but also as a symbol of pride and confidence.

our ancestors and we should respect them.

When someone dies people feel very sad. The relatives mourn for almost a week. People lose a lot of tears, and sometimes men lose control and they cry like ladies. People have to bury the body within hours, but it is important for our people to see somebody before they are in the grave, so everybody is led to see him or her (the deceased) *before being in the grave. In our culture, people believe if you die,*

you go to Heaven. They also think that if somebody dies, the spirit of the soul sometimes comes back to the family if people were not taking very good care of the person who died.

I was not religious when I was young, but I am now Christian. Today, I go to the church every Sunday to listen to the bible and sometimes I read some scriptures. I believe god is there – that's what I know. I pray hard."

RELIGION AND CULTURE IN SUDAN

When Arabs entered Sudan from Egypt some time after the 15th century, they brought their religion, Islam, with them. The indigenous people of the north adopted Islam, and some started speaking Arabic. The Arabs never reached the south of Sudan, where people practised traditional African religions, sometimes described as Animism. After Sudan became a British colony in the 19th century, missionaries converted many of the people of the south to Christianity. Today, the Arabic-speaking, Muslim north sees itself as part of the Middle East. The Black, Christian and Animist south, sees itself, along with much of Africa, as part of the English-speaking world.

SHARIA LAW

In 1983, Sharia law (Islamic law) was introduced in Sudan. Under Sharia law, crimes are judged in accordance with the Qu'ran (the holy book of Islam). Alcohol and gambling are prohibited and imprisonment is largely replaced by the death sentence or amputation (such as cutting off criminals' hands). Sharia law was abolished in 1985,

but re-introduced in 1991. However, it was not applied to the southern states of Equatoria, Bahr-el-Ghazal and Upper Nile. But it was applied to people from the south who are living in the north.

A Muslim man strings prayer beads at the entrance of the Grand Mosque in Khartoum.

CHAPTER TWO: The War Comes

As the civil war intensified, civilians soon became caught up in the conflict. People went hungry when fighting stopped them from sowing or harvesting their crops; villages were attacked by soldiers from both sides; homes and belongings were burned, and men, women and children killed. The war and subsequent famines were to claim the lives of one out of every five southern Sudanese.

CARBINO SAYS ...

I was first aware of the troubles in my country in 1983, when the Arabs, the militia, they came and raided our grazing place. That was when I maybe first realised that there was something wrong in my country. Everybody was informed by their community chiefs that we are fighting with

Arabs and they are coming. I heard some stories, especially in Eastern Upper Nile, that people were killing each other, tribal problems. It was caused by the Sudan government, though, changing the mentality of the civilians around – you are my people, those people are not your people, and so on. Making people fight each other.

A village burns. Soldiers on both sides of the conflict would often target everyone in a town or village, whether they were soldiers, supporters or innocent bystanders.

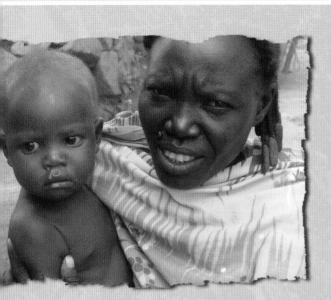

When villages were attacked, people saw family members, friends and neighbours injured, raped, or killed.

A lot of things happened. First it was the burning of the houses. Our village was burned three times. Those incidents cost a lots of lives, especially the old people who didn't have the strength to run, they were killed. And the young children and even women – a lot of people died during those incidents. I remember running – we would be running terribly; in the thorns, in the bushes. The soldiers would come and attack the village, especially at 4:00 am in the morning or sometimes at night, at midnight. Sometimes you didn't see them until they were just coming running up to you.

I heard about John Garang in 1984, when all the young men from the villages were mobilised to go to Ethiopia for guns. After they came back, they were describing John Garang as a king with a bald head, and he's very brave, and he's from a Dinka community."

KEY FIGURES IN THE WAR

The current President of Sudan, Umar al-Bashir, came to power on June 30, 1989. He was re-elected in 2000 for a five-year term. He has survived several coup attempts and tolerates little opposition or criticism.

• Since 1983, many people in the south have been represented by the Sudan People's Liberation Movement (SPLM) and its army, the Sudan People's Liberation Army (SPLA) led by John Garang. The Dinka people supported Garang, who wanted the south to remain in Sudan as a united but secular state.

• Between 1991 and 2002, there were several rival factions representing the people of the south. Garang's faction was known as the Torit faction. The rival leaders included William Nyuon Bany, Kerubino Kwanyin Bol and Rick Machar. They thought that the south should break away from Sudan and become an independent country.
The southern Nuer people supported the breakaway factions.

• There was fighting between the factions, and the government supplied some of the factions with arms.

John Garang is a Christian Dinka. He was educated in the USA.

"Everybody was worried – what will happen in the future, if things are getting worse very fast like this after a year? People were saying maybe it might stop, and some people were saying this thing might continue until more of the people will die and few will be alive. It was something that was unclear, and most of the people their perspective was that this war would continue for a long time because it was getting worse and worse and worse.

In the late 1980s, the SPLA had a meeting with all the community leaders, and the community leaders came back to the villages and started having meetings with the villagers. They told them the decision made by the SPLA, that they wanted to take the children for education to Ethiopia. It was not soldiers, but the community leaders who were organising the children. They went from house to house asking for boys.

I was feeling excited, but on the other hand I was really frightened. I was excited because this was not something for me alone, but for the young generation of my village. I saw that everybody was going, so I was having the motivation, that I should go also, so it was a bit like fun to me. Then I was frightened, because where we were going was very far and I had never experienced that long a walk.

I left the rest of my family living in the village. I had with me only a small blanket, my t-shirt and my shorts, plus tyre shoes – shoes made from a tyre. And I had a small gourd to carry water. I said goodbye to my mother and father. They were upset, especially my mother. She was very upset, she was really crying. She didn't say to me, I don't want you to go, but the way she looked, she was not happy at all for me to leave. I told them, you take good care of yourself, and also my brothers. Have a nice time, and maybe, hopefully, I see you again."

Carbino was just 11 years old when he left his village to go to Ethiopia – the same age as the young boy in this photo. There are no photographs of Carbino at this time.

Some of the boys who made the journey to Ethiopia were no more than six or seven years old.

THE LOST BOYS

In 1987, the civil war drove an estimated 20,000 young boys from their families and villages in southern Sudan. Some were orphans who had seen their families killed, others had been separated from their families as they escaped the fighting or fled from their burning villages. Many (like Carbino) were taken from their villages by SPLA soldiers to go to Ethiopia for safety, education or to be trained as soldiers. The groups of boys eventually reached Ethiopia, were then forced back into Sudan, and finally made it to safety in Kenya. They walked a thousand miles and many died. The survivors became known to the world as the 'Lost Boys of Sudan'.

CHILD SOLDIERS

There are approximately 17,000 child soldiers in southern Sudan. Some are orphans; others have been abducted by armed forces of both sides as they pass through a village. Children as young as eight are brought up by soldiers and taught to fight and kill, when they should be with their families and going to school. They have seen, and often done, terrible acts of violence and cruelty. The SPLA has now renounced the recruitment of child soldiers, and has worked with UNICEF to demobilise several thousand of them. One of the challenges of Sudan's peace will be to return these children to their families, provide them with the education they missed and help them adapt to normal life.

Children become soldiers in conflicts around the world. They are forced to kill and see their comrades die.

"When we started walking to Ethiopia, the boys from each village stayed together. From our village there were probably around 200 boys. The whole thing (the march) was maybe 2,000 to 3,000 boys. We walked for five to six hours every day. We started walking in the early evening and then we ended at around midnight. We slept where we stopped, in the bush. We walked at night because we were hiding from the militia. They were the Nuer people, who were against the SPLA. They were also against those leaving home for Ethiopia for education or training, like us. Once when the militias came at night, we were terrified. They found that we were young children and they were really aggressive to the few soldiers who were escorting us. We were not shot, but some of them were slapping boys and not showing a good mood to them.

People carried sorghum and we had one cup of food each day. Sometimes we stayed three or four days without food, so people just gathered food around. There was a lot of bush and some boys had spears and they went for fish. Eastern Upper Nile to the border has a lot of swamps, so we had water. People did not die from lack of water, but from lack of enough food. You get sick and then you just die very quickly because you don't have enough strength.

On the march, we were always told to keep going onwards and not back. The soldiers would say, you are under our protection, we can defend you. But if you go back

Carrying their few belongings, boys from southern Sudan march north towards Ethiopia.

by yourself, maybe you die alone without enough food or without care from somebody, so it's more dangerous for you to go back. Some of the boys ran away after a few days, but after a month it was difficult for people to go back home because we had covered a distance.

Some of the boys who didn't have shoes got blisters, which made it difficult to push ahead, and some of the boys started having a lot of nightmares. They were running around – they had mental problems. Some boys just died from diarrhoea and things like that. I did not know about malaria at that time. People got malaria because we walked in the water and we slept where there was no good bedding (mosquito nets); so, most of the people got infected from mosquitoes.

I was feeling strange, with body ache. I don't know if it was malaria or body ache from the long walk.

I saw quite a lot of boys die. It was really terrifying because you think that maybe tomorrow or next month you will be like that. They weren't my friends, but boys that I knew from our village – they lost their life."

WARFARE IN SUDAN – THE WEAPONS

The government forces in Sudan had tanks, planes and helicopters. Their soldiers on the ground had rifles and machine guns. The rebel forces were more lightly armed, but they also had rifles and machine guns. Both sides used mines to protect themselves from attack.

WARFARE IN SUDAN – THE TACTICS

The government forces controlled most of the towns, airfields and other important places such as the oil-fields. The rebels operated in the countryside and made sudden, unpredictable attacks on government forces and government-held areas. From time to time, the government forces waged an all-out attack on an area to try to drive the rebels out altogether. But in an area as big as southern Sudan, it was easy for the rebels to escape. The result was a stalemate – neither side could win.

SPLA (Sudan People's Liberation Army) soldiers practise drills prior to a visit by their leader, John Garang.

CHAPTER THREE: Life in a Refugee Camp

Refugee camps can be set up by the government of a country at war, by the governments of neighbouring countries or by international aid organisations. Sometimes camps simply evolve when many hundreds or thousands of desperate people converge on an area they hope will be safe. People fleeing fighting in the south of Sudan escaped to camps both within Sudan and over the borders in countries such as Ethiopia, Kenya and Uganda.

CARBINO SAYS ...

I did not know I was going to a refugee camp. I didn't know what a refugee camp was. People were telling us you are going to Ethiopia. My expectations were that maybe I'm going to a place like my home, like the way my village was.

My first impressions of the Etang refugee camp were ... you know ... the camp was not a very good camp. A lot of people around and sanitation was very poor. People defecated around – a lot of flies. It was smelly, very bad. The camp was very overcrowded. To me it was terrifying because I was looking at the Ethiopians and they looked like northern Sudanese, like Arabs, and I was terrified.

Ethiopia 1988: refugee boys at the Fugnido refugee camp in western Ethiopia. Most have severe malnutrition after their arduous trek from southern Sudan.

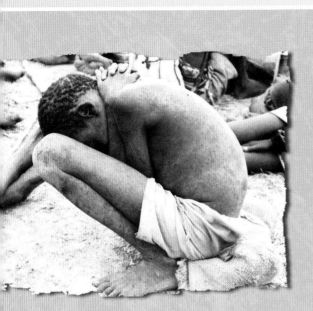

One of the Sudanese 'Lost Boys' at a refugee camp. Thousands of children lost one or both of their parents during the war – sometimes witnessing their death.

I was terrified of Arabs at that time.

They took us to a registration centre where our names were registered and they gave us food. We lived in thatched houses – tukuls. But big with a lot of boys, maybe 18 to 20 people in a tukul. We were given beds – it was the first bed I had ever slept in. The bed was made of wire and it was noisy. I could not sleep the first time, but I got used to it. There was no mattress, but the distributors from UNHCR (a branch of the United Nations dedicated to looking after refugees) gave you blankets and sheets. The food was flour, with powdered milk and lentils and oil. We collected our food at the storehouse every 15 days, and we went to the river to fetch water for food and to have a wash. There were no adults looking after us, we were looking after ourselves."

REFUGEE CAMPS – THE LOGISTICS

Refugee camps can house a few thousand people or hundreds of thousands of people. They are usually located on the outskirts of towns or cities.

• Shelters are built by the refugees or aid workers using any available materials – tree branches, metal sheets or plastic sheeting. Sometimes aid organisations provide tents.

• Access to water is essential. Water from wells, bore-holes (holes drilled deep in the ground) or springs is safe to use. Water collected from rivers or lakes needs to be filtered and have a chlorine solution added to kill off water-borne diseases such as cholera.

• Simple latrines (pits in the ground) are dug to be used as toilets. When a latrine is full, the pit is closed and a new one dug. Management of human waste is essential to stop the spread of diseases such as dysentery and cholera.

• Most camps have a clinic where health workers, who may be refugees, try to keep the people well, by vaccinating children against common diseases and helping those with malnutrition.

It is important that refugees are able to obtain culturally acceptable and familiar food in a camp.

23

"Personally for me it was a bit boring in the camp. I was thinking about back home, and there was no entertainment for me, except for sometimes we went swimming in the river, or we played games in the water. I was one of the youngest around. My uncle's sons were there taking good care of us. They were 18 or 19 years of age. They did most of the cooking. I also had my friend from my village, called Simon.

I saw boys defecating all the time – they had diarrhoea a lot. People had diarrhoea a lot, even me. Malaria cases were there, too, because we didn't have mosquito nets and there was a lot of water around the camp. We were told to go to the health centres within the camp. I saw quite a few white people working in the camp, in the health centres and even in the distribution centres. At that time communication was difficult because I had no English. After a few months, I began to learn English when they opened the schools. They brought in teachers and I started my English lessons and mathematics. Our teachers were Ethiopian.

After a few months in the camp I was not feeling very happy. I had travelled a long distance and I felt I couldn't return. I wondered how I could go back on foot alone. I thought maybe once I was older, I could think of going back alone, but it was something for the future.

A lot of people were dying in the camp. I saw a lot, a lot of people. Their bodies were buried. There were cemeteries around, far away from the camp where they took the dead bodies. The organisers of the camp paid people, the refugees, to bury the dead.

It was difficult in the camp, because there was no communication, no letters, no radios. Sometimes soldiers going home to southern Sudan from training centres in Ethiopia passed near the camp and boys heard some news from them – we are going to this

In most cases, refugees receive less than 10 litres of water per person per day, instead of the minimum emergency standard of 15 litres per person per day. An average adult in the UK or USA uses around 450 litres each day.

town for fighting, or there is fighting in this place. One day, it was announced to us in the school that there is a war in Ethiopia. (The Ethiopian government was fighting the people of Eritrea who wanted independence from Ethiopia).

When the information first came, people stayed in the camp, but after a few days people started leaving. At this time I had been in the camp four years and I was 15 years old."

DAILY LIFE IN A REFUGEE CAMP

Newly arrived refugees put up shelters, or register with the camp officials so that they can collect rations. Children play – often with toys they have made themselves – or go to school. The school may be well-equipped, or the pupils may sit under a tree and write with sticks in the dust. People grow crops on any little patch of land that they can find, or they may rent land or work on farms belonging to local people. Children collect water from wells, or hand-pumps. Women cook meals, using home-grown food, rations from aid organisations or food they have bought from local people. Men and boys scour the countryside for firewood.

LIVES LIVED IN CAMPS

Refugee camps are only meant to be temporary solutions, but for many, the problems that drove them away from their homes are not easily resolved. Many refugees find themselves living in camps for decades, and camp life becomes normal life. Babies are born, and old people die. There are jokes, laughter, games, music, dance, worship, love, fear and worry. Are we safe? Will we get enough to eat? When will we be able to go home? How are the people we left behind?

In Sudan, many children have been born and brought up in refugee camps. They have never known any other life.

Sudanese refugee women and children line up for the distribution of milk at a UNICEF-assisted feeding centre.

"So, we were getting evacuated. We were not actually attacked in the camp, but the enemies who would attack were a distance of only two hours away when we moved. They were Eritrean. We were to walk to the border of Sudan and Ethiopia. The walk was very difficult because it was in July, so the rivers around were full of water and the roads were flooded. So we were walking in the mud, carrying our luggage and food. We had to go a distance of two days walk to cross the border.

So we went up to the border, and the border is marked with a river (the River Gilo), and that river was full of water. All the refugees, young boys and women and everybody, were down on the banks of the river waiting to cross, and the river was full – a very heavy current. So, we stayed there for two days on the bank of the river, with heavy rain and no shelter. After two days, we were informed by one of the SPLA military commanders, who was there with the SPLA soldiers who were guiding the refugees, that the enemy is now a distance of two hours away from this place, so everybody should hurry to cross the river.

So, if you didn't know how to swim, you tried by all means to cross to the other side. There was a delay because the river was flooded and the current was so strong, so people could not … there was a great fear.

People delayed to the last moment, until the attacking started and the enemies (the Eritreans) started shooting people. Everybody was just jumping into the river with their clothes on. Those who knew how to swim and those who didn't. Thousands of people drowned at that river.

So me, personally, I removed my t-shirt and trousers and I jumped in with my underwear. I dived down under the water so that maybe I could escape the bullets. I raised my head out of the water for air three times. The fourth time, I hit the bank on the other side with my head. So I thought, I've made it. (The river was 100 metres wide.)

The enemy was shooting people in the river. The Eritreans were still on the side we left. Around the river there were big trees. Some of the enemy climbed the trees with their machine guns, AK47s, and they were just *shooting people in the river. So when I saw people shooting like that I decided to stay in the water. I stayed in the water from 3 pm to 9 pm. They stopped firing at 8 pm, then everything was quiet.*

Later, when I went to the next camp, one of the things I understood from the elders was that the people (the Eritreans) were not intending to shoot us. They were annoyed with the SPLA, because the SPLA government was supporting the Mengistu government in Ethiopia.

The majority of people died from the first bank to the second bank. When I reached the other side, I found a lot of people, most of them dead, shot. Some were half dead, half alive, they were crying. It was very dark. Afterwards when we reached Pachala Camp, everywhere people were mourning that they are missing people, especially the boys. Mourning the boys. They lost their brothers. And most of the people also lost were women, with young children who could not swim."

THE ATROCITIES OF WAR

Sudan's civil war has been marked by atrocities. Both sides have massacred civilians, abducted people and attacked aid workers. Soldiers have raped women and girls as young as eight years old. When rival factions of the Southern side fought each other, they were equally ruthless. Both sides looted food aid, and attacked places where aid agencies were providing relief to people affected by the war. The SPLA attacked and looted a relief station in Nyal in February, 2001. Government helicopter gunships attacked a relief station at Bieh in February, 2002, leading to the death of at least 24 people and the wounding of dozens of others.

LANDMINES

Landmines are small explosive devices that are hidden just underground. They explode when someone steps on them – whether that person is a soldier or a child. Between 1983 and 1999, landmines are estimated to have injured or killed 70,000 people in Sudan. When a conflict ends in a particular area, mines can only be removed by trained experts. Today, in around 70 countries, including Sudan, approximately 110 million unexploded landmines lie in wait.

A Sudanese landmine victim watches friends, also disabled by landmines, take part in a wheelchair basketball game at the Kakuma Refugee Camp in Kenya.

Refugee Camp - *Carbino's Story*

"When I got out of the river there was nobody. They had all gone. I was one of the last. There was a big path where all the people had gone, so I followed the path. I was feeling really terrified because I had seen a lot of deaths and I was really scared by the bombing and shelling. After two hours, I found some soldiers (SPLA) coming back to the place (the river). They asked me, who are you? And they asked me whether anybody was coming behind me? I told them, I don't know. They told me, okay you should go to be with the other people. After an hour in the direction they showed me, I met with some of the other boys. Some were wounded and they were carried by the soldiers. At midnight, we met up with everybody else. It was raining all the time and I had only underpants on when I got out of the river. One of the soldiers gave me one of his shirts and that was the thing I covered myself with.

After two days, everybody was together. We realised we were missing quite big numbers. In our group we were missing at least 20 to 30 boys, from our group of 55 boys.

(The refugees then walked to the Pachala Camp on the Sudanese side of the border.) I cannot remember a proper meal I had in that camp. The Red Cross came after one to two weeks. First they took the injured people, then they came back with some mosquito nets and plastic sheets,

Sudanese boys from the Etang Refugee Camp in Ethiopia following their crossing of the border back into Sudan.

Many African countries are at war – here refugees in Uganda, fleeing attacks by the Lord's Resistance Army (LRA), strip a tree for firewood in a camp for IDPs.

NEIGHBOURS IN WAR

Refugees from Sudan's civil war have fled to neighbouring countries for safety, but many of those countries have wars and refugees of their own.

• At the end of 2003, the UNHCR's statistical yearbook recorded 606,242 Sudanese refugees living in neighbouring African countries. There were over 100,000 refugees from Eritrea, Ethiopia, Uganda, Chad and the Democratic Republic of Congo living in Sudan.

• In Uganda, there has been a long-running rebellion by a force known as the Lord's Resistance Army (LRA). Most experts agree the LRA is supported by the government of Sudan. The LRA attacks villages and abducts young people to be used as soldiers. It also attacks camps in Uganda that are housing refugees from southern Sudan.

• In the Democratic Republic of Congo there has been a civil war, with many neighbouring countries involved, since 1995.

• In Ethiopia there had been a 30-year war between the government and the people of Eritrea. The war ended in 1993, and Eritrea became an independent country. The Ethiopian government supported the SPLA in Sudan.

• Thousands of Sudanese people who sought refuge in neighbouring countries were caught up in those countries' internal conflicts. The largest group of refugees from southern Sudan – some 223,000 – is in Uganda. Another 88,000 refugees are in Ethiopia; 69,000 in the Democratic Republic of Congo; 60,000 in Kenya; an estimated 36,000 in the Central African Republic; and 30,000 in Egypt.

and some food. They distributed some grain to us, but it was not enough. You just got some grain in your hand and you ate that little bit, twice a day. People were going outside the camp to sell things for food. It was a part of Sudan, so there were Sudanese living around. You could sell your own clothes for food – anything.

After some time in this camp, we were hearing that this place is not good. Maybe later in the dry season the Sudan government will come and attack this place, or Eritreans will come and attack this place. But I was not really able to get information of where was safe to go. So, I stayed in the camp."

CHAPTER FOUR: The 'Lost Boys'

After their terrible experiences in Ethiopia, the 'Lost Boys' spent some time in the Pachala Camp before wandering Sudan for several months. Finally, with the help of the UNHCR (the Office of the United Nations High Commissioner for Refugees), they were transported to the Kakuma refugee camp in Kenya.

CARBINO SAYS ...

"After I left Ethiopia I suffered a lot. From Pachala camp we left the border area to walk to eastern Equatoria. It was November, 1991. On the third day we were attacked and 16 boys were killed at night. After seven days we were visited by UNHCR representatives. They sent trucks and we were transported to Narus, to the Kenyan border on the Sudanese side.

We stayed there for three months. But then the Sudan government captured Kapoeta, which was only four hours from where we were. So, the UNHCR said we should walk to Kenya. We started from Narus to Lokichoggio, where we camped for two months. Then the UNHCR took us to the Kakuma camp in Kenya.

In Kakuma, they wanted to mix us. We should not live as brothers from the same village because it may create tribal problems. They said we want to mix you to be friends with others. So we were mixed. I was living with other boys, from all over Sudan. Not just Dinka.

The 'Lost Boys' board UNHCR trucks to go to the Kakuma camp in Kenya.

HUMANITARIAN AID

International aid agencies help refugees and IDPs by supplying them with food, water supplies, shelter and health care. The war in Sudan has made it difficult for aid agencies to provide this help. The fighting may make it dangerous or impossible to reach people in need. It may also be hard to ensure that the aid gets to the people who need it most, and not just those, especially soldiers, who are able to take it. Finally, each side may be reluctant to allow aid to reach the people in areas controlled by the other side.

A Médecins Sans Frontières (Doctors Without Borders) plane lands in a remote part of Sudan. MSF doctors and workers are providing medical care across Sudan.

THE EMOTIONAL EFFECTS OF WAR

How does it feel to be a refugee? Different people have different experiences, but some of the feelings will be common. Fear when your village or family is attacked. Grief for loved ones who have been killed, or who you have lost touch with in the chaos of escape. Worry: will you reach safety? Will the place you reach stay safe? Will you be re-united with the rest of your family? And anger about what has happened to you, and at the soldiers who destroyed your life.

Many survivors of war feel guilt about surviving when so many others didn't.

For a while we stayed in an open area without shelters. They made open latrines so we could go to the toilet and there were hand pumps for water. They created this camp for us, and bit by bit they built us houses and a school. In 1993, we resumed our education. We learned English, mathematics, science, agriculture as well as geography and civics, talking about cultures. Our teachers were Kenyans. I stayed for eight years in that camp.

The food situation was really frustrating, no changes, just sorghum, oil and lentils. That's the only food for eight years. It was very difficult. There was not enough food. You had 9 kilos for 15 days. Our food was from UNHCR."

"We lived in a tukul of six people. There was one room with six beds, an iron sheet door and a small, small window. There was a hand pump and one shared kitchen for about 80 to 90 people. I was living with four boys from different parts of Sudan, Atem Nyok from Gogarail, Satino Mabek and Simon Majak from Panaru and Peter Mac from Bor. Sometimes we got into some arguments because nobody was cleaning the room or someone did not take their turn to fetch water. But apart from those small things, we got along most of the time, friend to brother supporting each other.

I had learned football in Ethiopia, so when I reached Kenya, I was a bit professional! In the camp there were competitions between schools and we were given playing equipment like boots and shin-guards, but for school use, not personal use.

Kakuma is one of the biggest camps with six nationalities living there. It was first inhabited by the Sudanese, then came the Ethiopians. The Sudanese and Ethiopians got along, but there were problems when the Somalians came in. They are very traditional with their religion (Islam) and things like that. Many of the Sudanese people in the camp were Christian, so it was a Christian/Muslim problem. People ended up fighting sometimes in the market in Kakuma town or in the small markets in the camps. People also attacked each other. You might get some Sudanese boys who like to rape a young Somalian girl, or Somalian boys who want to rape young Sudanese girls, or boys who rob people and things like this. Also, there were the Kenyan natives, Turkanas. They were attacking boys of all nationalities at night, robbing them.

After seven years, that's when they killed my Simon. It was very sad, he was killed by two Turkanas. He went for a walk outside the camp and he met with two young Turkana boys, who normally have spears and knives. They started showing some bad behaviour and they speared him on the head. After that he had internal bleeding in the brain. People came and they found Simon.

Many refugees live with terrible memories of things they have experienced and seen.

He was still alive, but he was unconscious. They brought him to one of the health centres. So we went there and we found him. They took him in an ambulance to the Red Cross hospital in the camp.

He was taken for an operation, but after one day we heard that he had died. I was feeling really bad to Turkanas after that, towards the natives around."

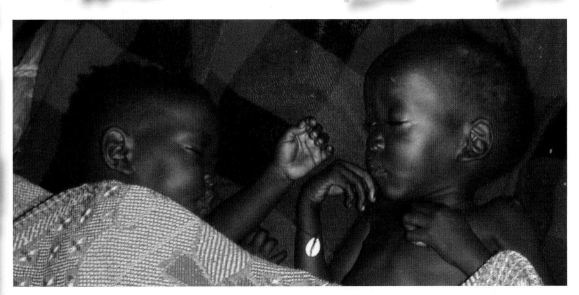

Even if they are still with their families and in their home village, many children in Sudan have been hungry for most of their lives – 21 per cent of Sudan's population is malnourished.

FAMINE IN SUDAN

Like many countries in Africa, Sudan suffers droughts. Severe drought can lead to crop failure, also farm animals starve when they cannot find enough to eat. When food runs out, people sometimes migrate to places where there is food or work. Or they may have to rely on food brought to them by aid organisations. However, war makes both these options difficult. An estimated 570,000 people have died of hunger in southern Sudan during the years of war. There were droughts and famines from 1984 to 1985, the early 1990s and again in 1998, and 2001.

THE OIL INDUSTRY

Oil was discovered at Bentiu in southern Sudan in 1978. In 1998, a pipeline from the oil-field to Sudan's Red Sea coast was started, and in 1999 oil began to flow and Sudan started to export it. This had two effects on the war. One was that oil provided the government with more money to fight the war. The second effect was that the oil-wells and the pipeline became important strategic targets. Government troops have displaced hundreds of thousands of people from the oil-fields, destroying crops and homes to try to make sure that no-one returns.

Refugee Camp - *Carbino's Story*

"In 1998, I found out it could be possible to go to America. There was an agreement between the UNHCR and the American government to take young boys to America for education and a better life than in the camp. In the beginning I didn't know anything about America, but the Sudanese who were applying were being orientated before they left the camp – they were teaching you what is in America, American culture, lots of things.

In 1999, we filled in the forms and our interviews and photos were attached to our forms. But in 2000, there was still no proper news about the process and I thought maybe it will not happen, so I forgot about the American thing. Eventually, though, thousands of boys went.

I know most of the boys who went to America – my friends in the school and in the groups where we were living. I haven't talked with anybody

directly, but I have heard from people, who communicate with them, that they have a better life. The majority of the boys get higher studies, have a good education or they are working. But most of them would like to come back, particularly now that there is peace in Sudan.

I thought about my family back home and I tried to have communication, but I couldn't until 2000. That's when ICRC (the International Committee of the Red Cross) helped me and the other boys through their tracing facilities. Most of the boys heard news about their family before I heard, and they heard sad news that they had lost all their family. So I was in a really big dilemma. Maybe I might be getting the news that there's nobody there. I was feeling very bad about some of my friends who lost their family. The only thing we could do was to help each other and help ourselves

Some of the 'Lost Boys' on a plane for the first time. They are flying from Kakuma to Nairobi before finally returning home to Sudan.

to deal with the situation.

In the camp, us boys were like brothers. We were staying together always, everybody understanding the other one.

There were 22,000 boys originally. Some boys joined the SPLA military, others died during all those problems. By the end, in Kakuma there were 16,000 boys – 6,000 boys were lost."

A young child stands alone in a Sudanese refugee camp in the Darfur region of Sudan. Thousands of children have been orphaned by the war.

THE HUMAN COST OF WAR

All wars are cruel, but the long-running civil war has taken a terrible toll on the people of Sudan.

• An estimated average of 300 people have died each day, day after day, for 21 years.

• During the war, at least 85 per cent of the inhabitants of southern Sudan were displaced at least once.

• At least 115 times in just one year (2000) Sudanese government planes deliberately dropped bombs on towns, villages, hospitals, schools, health clinics, displacement camps and relief food distribution centres in Sudan -– locations with absolutely no military significance.

• During an offensive against the SPLA in March and April 1992, the government ordered aid flights to stop for six weeks.

• One in seven of Sudan's population is a displaced person or a refugee. Sudan has the biggest population of displaced people of any country in the world. One of every nine refugees in the world is from Sudan.

• In 2000, United Nations agencies estimated that more than 50,000 children in southern Sudan had lost both their parents as a consequence of the civil war.

"Finally, I had a message from the Red Cross that my family were alive. They had left our home and gone to Khartoum. They sent me a letter: if you are still there in the camp, you look for a means of coming to Khartoum. I was very happy. I wanted to go back to Sudan to see my parents again because it had been a long time, 14 years, without anybody. I applied to one of the repatriation offices in the camp and I was accepted to be repatriated back to Khartoum. When I left Kakuma in 2000 I was 22 years old.

My journey back to Sudan was very nice. The UNHCR gave me pocket money and they paid for my ticket on a plane to Khartoum. That was my first chance to take a plane. A big plane with a lot of different people, and there were only five boys, young Sudanese, so everybody was very interested in us and where we were going. I was feeling very proud in that plane, because most of the people in that plane were foreigners coming to Khartoum, and I was speaking with them in English. I was sitting next to an old man and he was asking me what kind of career I have and why I am in this plane to Khartoum. So I gave him a short life story of mine and he was a bit shocked. But that's how it was!

So I reached Khartoum at night. In the morning I took the bus to the town where my parents were and I found my cousin and my aunt. When I arrived at the house, my mum and my dad were out and I found only James, Moses was at school. When I'd left, James was still very young, so my aunt and cousin were telling him this is your brother Carbino. He had heard a lot about me from my mum, but he was very young when I left him. He was just looking at me, as if I was a stranger and after that he sat crying. All of us cried. After some hours, my mum and my dad came back and then everybody was crying in the house! I didn't tell them I was coming, I just started my process very quietly in Kenya, so it was a shock, a sudden visit. After that my father slaughtered a cock because in our culture if somebody arrives in the house you kill something and then after a day we slaughtered the goat, a big male, for my welcoming party, to celebrate.

A few years back I had said to my family that I hope to see you again. It had been 14 years, but I made it to see them again."

Like many southern Sudanese, Carbino's family had actually moved north managing to find safety in Khartoum. Today, around 2 million internally-displaced people are still living on the outskirts of Khartoum in IDP camps or in the city's slums. They live like the other poor people of the city on whatever low-paid work they can find.

REFUGEES' RIGHTS

Under international law, refugees have rights to protection and support. People who have a well-founded fear of persecution in their own country have the right, under the 1951 UN Refugee Convention, to seek asylum in a different country. People fleeing war can also be considered refugees. UNHCR is responsible for looking after refugees, including some internally displaced persons. Most of the world's refugees do not flee very far and live over the border in neighbouring countries.

'Lost Boy', Peter Nyarol Dut celebrates his upcoming journey to America in the Kakuma refugee camp.

While completing his studies in the USA, Peter Nyarol Dut supports himself with a job at Wal Mart.

THE LOST BOYS IN THE USA

In 2001, nearly 4,000 'Lost Boys' went to the United States seeking peace, freedom and education. The boys have had mixed fortunes, but most have found it harder than they had expected. Those who were under 18 went to school, and some are now at university working for degrees and qualifications. Those who were over 18, had to get jobs, and without qualifications they could only find low-paid work. Some of them have continued their education in their spare time. Those who have relations still in the refugee camp are sending money back to Kenya.

CHAPTER FIVE: Looking to the future

After they were reunited, Carbino's family decided to go back to southern Sudan so that Carbino's father could continue farming. The family moved to Dilling, where they were able to buy some land and start again.

CARBINO SAYS ...

"After one year back in southern Sudan I decided to go back to Khartoum because I was interested in going to one of the universities to be a teacher. I applied and they accepted me. But then they told me you will have to be trained to be a soldier and go into the Sudan military for two years. After that you can join your university. So it was a difficult decision for me. They mainly send people for fighting to southern Sudan, so I decided not to do that because I could be fighting my own people, and there was a high possibility I could die. So, I went to the Nuba Mountains and became a teacher with NRRDO (Nuba Relief, Rehabilitation and Development Organization) in Kauda.

In May 2002, I began working with Médecins Sans Frontières. They were looking for translators around this region and they submitted a letter to the regional governor. That man knows me and he decided I would be the right person to do the translation job with MSF.

I now live in the eastern mountains in a small village called Limun where MSF are based. In my typical day with MSF, I start in the morning at 8 am with meetings between regional staff and international staff, translating. Then I work with the doctor, doing the ward rounds and looking at the patients. After that I may go with the doctor to the tuberculosis (TB) centre, or to the consulting room or

Carbino translates during a meeting between local and international MSF staff.

Carbino and his colleagues from a Médecins Sans Frontières team currently working in the Nuba Mountains.

MSF WORLDWIDE

Médecins Sans Frontières (Doctors Without Borders) have been providing emergency medical assistance to populations in danger since 1971. They are currently working in more than 80 countries. MSF teams will often travel to places that many people have never heard of, raising awareness of crisis situations. MSF maintains neutrality and independence from individual governments, and the majority of its funds come from donations from the general public.

MSF IN SUDAN

MSF has been helping people in both northern and southern Sudan since 1979. They provide basic health care at hospitals and through networks of clinics and health centres. They treat people with diseases such as tuberculosis and malaria; they provide food and treat the severely malnourished; they run vaccination programmes and provide sanitation facilities and clean water. There are currently 282 international MSF staff and 3,657 local staff (like Carbino) working in Sudan.

with the nurses in the health centre. I translate English into Arabic and Arabic into English. I travel a lot, to the different places where MSF are working. This job is interesting and you learn a lot of things from different people, especially on the medical side. In my job it motivates me to listen to the mothers and to be able to give their stories to the doctors so they can help the children.

(Carbino also spends a lot of his spare time talking and playing football with the orphaned children who live in the region where he works.) *The children take me back to my life. I tell them about my life: I was like you, but you see my life has changed. I have been moved from home to a different place and now I am an adult. I have an education and I am now working here. If you keep on encouraging yourself and go to school every day and learn football, you might be a footballer in life, or a good teacher or a good doctor."*

"I wanted to be a teacher, that was my ambition. But now I don't have a final decision on what to do. I have been involved in medical activities for three years with MSF, so I learn a lot of medical stuff. For a job in education, I need to go to college to be trained professionally as a teacher. It will maybe take two years. That's the system in Kenya anyway, and nowadays maybe in southern Sudan. Everything is getting calm now, so I think there might be a chance of doing this.

I think Sudan could be a peaceful country. If there's peace in Sudan there will be access to development. Then there might be free movement of immigration in Sudan and the outside world might visit, and people will want to run businesses in Sudan. You know, the world can help Sudan if there's peace. The donors in the world will think the money will be spent wisely if there is no war. The money will be used in development – building schools, roads, hospitals, water facilities and rebuilding the places that have been destroyed during the war.

I do worry for my future. I worry how I am going to manage because my life is still very basic. I don't have enough support financially, so it creates a very big worry. How am I going to get more? Be more settled? I want to have a wife and kids, two or three, and I want to have a better education.

The saddest day of my life was the time when I lost my Simon in the refugee camp. I was very, very sad. The happiest day of my life was when I met again with my younger brothers and with my mum and dad after 14 years.

What's my most precious possession? I don't have a lot of good things but I like the picture of my girlfriend. She's called Achol John. She's quite beautiful.

Carbino relaxes with MSF colleagues after completing the interviews for this book.

What helped me to survive are some words from my father. He told me when I was young, you are born as a man. Don't panic with small stuff and always have courage with you, even though you face problems. It made me simplify everything. Any problem in my life, I just encouraged myself that these are the things that I have to face as somebody living."

A new MSF tuberculosis (TB) clinic under construction in the village of Limun where Carbino lives and works.

HELPING SUDAN

Operation Lifeline Sudan was set up in 1989 and became the world's largest aid operation. It was led by the United Nations (UN) and was made up of 40 aid organisations and UN agencies. Through OLS, hundreds of thousands of people in Sudan were helped during the war. In the future, the challenge will be to help the people of Sudan rebuild their country and their lives. Aid organisations will need to work with communities in areas such as water provision, education, health care infrastructure and income generation. In areas devastated by fighting, homes will need to be rebuilt, crops planted and landmines cleared.

THE END OF WAR IN SOUTHERN SUDAN

The United Nations, the European Union, and the USA have all put pressure on the government of Sudan to bring the civil war to an end. Neighbouring countries have taken in refugees, in some cases they have supported the SPLA, and encouraged peace talks. In January 2005, after many years of negotiations, the two sides in the civil war signed a peace agreement.

As this book goes to print (in spring 2005), there seem to be reasonable prospects for peace in southern Sudan, after 21 years of war, destruction and suffering. To date, some 600,000 spontaneous returnees (200,000 non-registered refugees and 400,000 IDPs) have already gone back to southern Sudan on their own. Another 550,000 refugees are still in neighbouring countries and 6.1 million IDPs remain uprooted in the devastated region.

In an operation that will last some years, UNHCR plans to voluntarily repatriate more than a million refugees. But a great deal of assistance is required, particularly in light of the lack of roads and basic services in the south.

CHAPTER SIX: Darfur and Sudan's future

Darfur is a large state in the west of Sudan. It is home to nomadic, Arab camel-herders and settled Black farmers who have converted to Islam. It is far from the war in southern Sudan, but as peace approached in the south, Darfur was plunged into war. In February 2003, rebels in Darfur rose up against the government, claiming that the region was being neglected by the government in Khartoum.

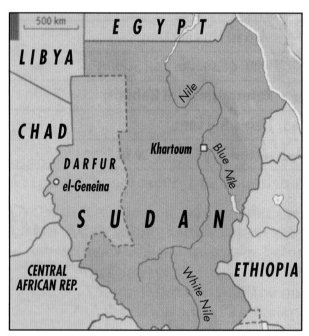

Darfur is a dry, rocky region in the west of Sudan.

REBELLION AND REFUGEES

The revolt may have been triggered by the moves towards peace in the south, and the hope that Darfur could gain similar rights to those that the south wanted.

In January, 2004, the army moved to put down the uprising. Along with Arab 'Janjaweed' militias, they attacked villages suspected of supporting the rebels. Tens of thousands were killed; 130,000 fled to refugee camps over the border in Chad; and over a million – a sixth of the region's population – were internally displaced. By the end of 2004, 1.8 million people were uprooted from their homes –

200,000 in refugee camps in Chad and 1.6 million internally displaced within Darfur.

ETHNIC CLEANSING OR GENOCIDE?

The scale of the killing and destruction soon drew the attention of the outside world. The United Nations (UN) began to be concerned that the government forces were not just attacking the rebels and their supporters, but may have been carrying out ethnic cleansing or genocide. The term ethnic cleansing, means that one ethnic group uses violence to drive another group out of its land. Genocide goes further – this is the attempt by one ethnic group to wipe out another entire ethnic group. It seemed to some observers that the Arabs of Darfur were trying to kill or expel all the Black people of the region. The government of

The army burned villages, stole cattle, destroyed wells and drove people from their homes in the Darfur region.

History repeats itself. Children in a refugee camp in Darfur live in shelters built from plastic sheets and cardboard boxes.

Sudan denied these allegations, and agreed to disarm the Janjaweed forces. But in September, 2004, a UN envoy said that the government had not met the targets for disarming the militia, and must accept outside help to protect civilians. The US Secretary of State, Colin Powell, described the killings in Darfur as genocide. Early in 2005, a UN report accused the government and militias of systematic abuses in Darfur, but stopped short of calling the violence genocide.

THE FUTURE FOR DARFUR

As this book goes to print (in spring 2005), fighting in Darfur continues and thousands of people are still displaced. The UN is putting pressure on the government of Sudan to control the Janjaweed forces, and hoping to send in a peace-keeping force.

AID FOR AFRICA

In the early months of 2005, the British Prime Minister, Tony Blair, made a priority of helping Africa. He set up a Commission, which reported on how increased aid, debt relief, fairer trade, and better government could help people in Africa escape poverty. He promised to use Britain's position in the G8 group of rich countries, and in the European Union, to press for more generous aid and the cancellation of debts owed by African countries. Everyone who cares about Africa agrees that peace is essential, in Sudan and in other African countries, for other measures to work. Peace enables aid to reach those who need it most. Peace frees up government resources for development and reconstruction. Peace means that people have the security to plan and invest for the future. With peace, and with help from richer countries, Africans can work their way out of poverty.

Asha Suleiman Ibrahim sifts sorghum bought in the east of Sudan by the World Food Programme. It was distributed to displaced people in Darfur.

43

In 2000, United Nations agencies estimated that 170,000 children in southern Sudan had no information about their biological parents. Many children have had to become mother and father to younger brothers and sisters.

A UN commission, sent to investigate allegations of killings, torture and rape in Darfur, has drawn up a list of 51 suspects. The list includes Sudanese government and army officials, as well as militia and rebel leaders. The UN has given the list to the International Criminal Court (ICC) to start prosecutions for war crimes.

THE PEACE DIVIDEND

International pressure helped bring peace to the south, and is now being applied to bring peace to Darfur. There are encouraging examples from other African countries which have emerged from years of civil war into peace. At first, the peace was fragile, but has now lasted for many years. Mozambique, and more recently Angola are good examples of a lasting peace which has made development possible. Most African countries contain a mixture of tribes with different languages, traditions and ways of life, and while many countries have a mixture of Muslim and Christian populations, people are able to live together in mutual toleration.

SUDAN – WAR AND POVERTY

Sudan is not the only poor country in Africa, but it has been made poorer than it need be by the war. Ninety-two per cent of the population live below the poverty line. Life expectancy at birth is between 55 and 60 years. Less than 25 per cent of the population of southern Sudan, and only about 60 per cent of people in the north, have access to safe water. Leprosy, river blindness, polio and other diseases are rife in southern Sudan, where only 30 to 40 per cent of people live within one day's walk of a health facility. At least one in ten children die before they reach five – this figure is closer to one in five in the south.

WHAT WOULD PEACE MEAN TO SUDAN?

Peace would bring many practical benefits to Sudan. The government was spending nearly £125 million every year on the war. Money that has been spent on the war would be available to rebuild the country and to pay for desperately needed education and health care. Peace would allow trade to take place – Sudan has many resources, especially oil, which could make everyone in the country better off. People would be able support themselves again by growing crops and raising animals. Aid agencies would be able to transfer resources from helping refugees to supporting long-term development. In time, people would be able to leave the refugee camps and go home.

A young, Sudanese refugee shelters from a dust storm in a refugee camp in Chad.

HOW YOU CAN HELP

Funds are desperately needed in Sudan: people living in refugee camps need food, clean water and medical care. Refugees who are now returning home, need help to build new houses, wells, schools and medical facilities, and help to restart their farms and start businesses.

1. MAKE A DONATION

You can donate as much or as little as you like to any official charity or aid organisation. Make sure it is a registered charity. Details of how to make a donation will be listed on individual organisation's websites – see page 47 for websites.

2. ORGANISE A FUNDRAISER

Engage the help of an adult and arrange for an event, clearly stating why you are raising money and for who.

3. BE INFORMED OF THE ISSUES

Watch the television news, read newspapers, check out the websites of official government and non-government organisations; most are regularly updated.

4. ASK AN ORGANISATION TO COME AND TALK AT YOUR SCHOOL

Generating greater awareness of the problems can really help. Many organisations offer this on their website.

5. SIGN AN ONLINE PETITION

There are many petitions on the Internet you can sign, to add your voice to those who are calling for more help for refugees around the world.

GLOSSARY

ADDIS ABABA PEACE AGREEMENT The agreement between the government of Sudan and the Anya Nya rebel movement in 1972, which ended the first civil war in southern Sudan. The agreement made the South a self-governing region of Sudan.

ANIMIST The traditional religions of the people of South Sudan. Carbino describes the beliefs of Dinka people on pages 14 and 15.

ANYA NYA The organisation which led the first revolt against the government of Sudan between 1956 and 1972.

CHOLERA A deadly infectious disease, caught by drinking water polluted with human waste. Vaccination can protect against cholera.

CIVILIANS Everyone who is not a member of the armed forces.

CIVIL WAR A war between different forces within a country. They may be fighting to gain control of the government, or one force may be fighting for independence for part of the country.

COUP The overthrow of an existing government by a group of rebels.

FAMINE When large numbers of people do not have enough to eat. Famines happen when crops fail, often because of a drought. They are made worse when people are too poor to buy food, when they cannot get to where there is food, and when food aid cannot reach the hungry people. In bad famines, many thousands of people die of hunger and disease.

DYSENTERY An infectious disease, caught by drinking water polluted with human waste. Bad cases can be fatal.

GENEVA CONVENTION Rules agreed by the world's governments about fighting wars, treating prisoners of war, and caring for refugees. The 1951 Geneva convention defines the rights of refugees.

HUMANITARIAN Humanitarian agencies are charities and international organisations which look after people affected by natural disasters, wars, and famines.

INTERNALLY-DISPLACED PERSONS (IDPS) People who have been forced to flee their homes because of war, but who have not crossed a border into another country.

JANJAWEED Armed groups fighting on the government side in Darfur, in Sudan, which are not official members of the government army.

LEPROSY An infectious disease. If untreated, it can cause disfigurement and disability.

MACHAKOS PROTOCOL The agreement between the SPLA and the government of Sudan, signed in Kenya in 2002, which started the peace process to end the war in South Sudan.

MALARIA A disease caused by parasites in the blood transmitted by the bite of mosquitoes.

MALNUTRITION Ill-health caused by not getting enough of the right kind of food. Eating food which lacks vitamins and protein can cause malnutrition.

NOMADIC People who continually move around and who have no permanent home.

POLIO An infectious disease which can cause disability. Vaccination can prevent polio.

REFUGEES People who have been forced to flee their homes and have crossed a border into a neighbouring country for safety. Often the word is used to also include internally-displaced persons.

RIVER BLINDNESS A disease which can cause blindness. It is caused by a tiny parasitic worm, transmitted by a small black fly.

SANITATION Safe, clean ways of dealing with human waste. Flush toilets, sewers, and sewage processing plants help to prevent disease in modern cities. In refugee camps, sanitation may be in the form of latrines.

SECULAR Non-religious. A secular state respects the religious beliefs of all its people, but does not have a state religion.

SHARIA LAW Law based on the Qu'ran, the holy book of Islam. Since 1991, Sharia law has applied in the north of Sudan.

SUDAN PEOPLE'S LIBERATION ARMY (SPLA) The main army fighting on behalf of the people of southern Sudan against the army of the government of Sudan.

TUBERCULOSIS An infectious disease, often affecting the lungs, which can be fatal. It can be prevented by vaccination, and treated by drugs.

UNHCR The Office of the United Nations High Commissioner for Refugees.

UNICEF The United Nations Children's Fund, an agency of the UN established to help governments improve the health, lives and education of the world's children.

UNITED NATIONS (UN) An international organisation of countries set up in 1945 to promote international peace, security and co-operation. Some of its functions today include working on social, educational and health issues.

FURTHER INFORMATION

ADOPT-A-MINEFIELD
"So that people whose lives are shattered by landmines can once again experience life to the full". www.landmines.org

AMNESTY INTERNATIONAL
A worldwide movement of people who campaign for internationally recognised human rights. www.amnesty.org

ICRC The International Committee of the Red Cross. www.icrc.org

MEDECINS SANS FRONTIERES
67-74 Saffron Hill, London, EC1N 8QX
020 7404 6600 www.uk.msf.org

OXFAM INTERNATIONAL
Works in more than 100 countries to find lasting solutions to poverty, suffering and injustice. www.oxfam.org.uk/coolplanet/index.htm

SAVE THE CHILDREN
An independent organisation creating real and lasting change for children in need. www.savethechildren.org

THE SAVE DARFUR COALITION
An alliance of over 100 faith-based, humanitarian and human rights organisations. www.savedarfur.org

UNHCR
The Office of the United Nations High Commissioner for Refugees. Within the UK, UNHCR's London office can provide educational resources, display materials, speakers, information on refugee issues worldwide and advice on fundraising. Most resources are free of charge. www.unhcr.ch

UNICEF
For further information on issues affecting children around the world. www.unicef.org